BOSTON
THEN & NOW

59 Boston Sites Photographed in the
Past and Present

Peter Vanderwarker
With the Assistance of the Boston Public Library

With a Foreword by
Robert Campbell

DOVER PUBLICATIONS, INC.
NEW YORK

Dedicated to
Peter Blake
Who first proposed the idea for this book

PHOTOGRAPHIC CREDITS

The Bostonian Society: 2, 12, 34, 44, 62, 63, 64, 66, 68, 78, 80.

The Society for the Preservation of New England Antiquities: 42, 76, 112, 120.

All other antique views are from the Boston Pictorial Archive, Print Department, the Boston Public Library.

Aerial photograph, page 3, by Alex S. McClean.

Copyright © 1982 by Peter Vanderwarker.
All rights reserved under Pan American and International Copyright Conventions.

Published in Canada by General Publishing Company, Ltd., 30 Lesmill Road, Don Mills, Toronto, Ontario.
Published in the United Kingdom by Constable and Company, Ltd.

Boston Then and Now: 59 Boston Sites Photographed in the Past and Present is a new work, first published by Dover Publications, Inc., in 1982.

Manufactured in the United States of America
Dover Publications, Inc.
31 East 2nd Street
Mineola, N.Y. 11501

Library of Congress Cataloging in Publication Data

Vanderwarker, Peter.
  Boston then and now.

  1. Boston (Mass.)—Buildings—Pictorial works.
2. Boston (Mass.)—Description—Views. 3. Historic sites
—Massachusetts—Boston—Pictorial works. 4. Architecture
—Massachusetts—Boston—Pictorial works. I. Title.
F73.37.V36   974.4'61   81-17385
ISBN 0-486-24312-5   AACR2

FOREWORD
by Robert Campbell

Peter Vanderwarker's photographs set the present and the past side by side, in paired images like two halves of one time-warped stereograph. It's instructive and even moving to read Peter's description of how he printed the contemporary set of views. He placed the historic print on the enlarging easel, then projected the negative of the contemporary scene onto it. The practical reason was to match the two perfectly in cropping and size. Yet there's a poetic metaphor at work too: the present is literally projected onto the past; the past shows through the present like the *pentimento* of a painting. In a time-layered city like Boston the past really does show through the present, creating most of the city's visual richness.

Yet a doubt remains. Can we ever really know the past? Aren't these paired pictures terribly misleading? Imagine the old-time photographer coming to his scene with his cumbersome equipment. He comes at dawn, when the streets are clear of the traffic he knows will show merely as a disfiguring blur because of the long exposure his film requires. The dawn light is soft. There are few people around and nothing kicks up the dust of the street. With leisure, the photographer composes his view. Or perhaps he waits till another day, when a parade will fill his street and bunting embellish its buildings.

A century or half-century later, Peter Vanderwarker comes to the same place but to a very different scene. The result of the earlier photographer's work is in his hand. It's midday, maybe, with bright sun and hard shadows making for much contrast, little repose. Cars and people clutter the street and obscure any sense of it as an urban space. And by the very act of imitation, so faithfully performed, Peter misleads in another sense. By adopting the exact framing and vantage point of the original view, which was carefully chosen and composed, Peter ensures, paradoxically, that his own composition can only be a random one. Where the old photographer picked a beautiful scene and framed it lovingly, Peter must photograph whatever he happens to find in front of his camera. He can choose neither his view nor the framing of it. It isn't surprising that the result is often chaos. Does this mean the city has become more chaotic? The answer is unknowable.

Yet with all these caveats, some lessons do emerge. The old city, it appears, was superior to the new in grain, human scale, continuity, urban space and in a quality I call face. The new city is superior to the old in comfort, convenience and visual drama.

Grain is the pepper-and-salt of small detail—signs on the building fronts, just for one example. And it's also the frequent (but not too big, not dramatic) variation in building height and style. Human scale is the sense the old buildings have that they're places for people. Their windows and doors and awnings and stoops and decorative elements are person-sized. Continuity means the way most of the architecture emerges from the same general classical tradition, a tradition that provides elements that carry over from one building to the next, knitting them together into one city fabric: roof cornices, windows expressed as framed rectangles punched into the building wall (so different from the glass strips or skins of recent years), rustications, solid masonry itself as the basic material.

Urban spaces are all those outdoor rooms—streets as corridors, squares as parlors—that made of the pedestrian city one huge public social club. In the automobile city, space is often shapeless and buildings are not its walls but merely objects in it. "Face" is harder to define, but you can't miss it in the old photos. The buildings are humanoid: windows suggest, as eyes do, intelligences behind them looking out; buildings have tops and bottoms like hats and boots. Lined up and jostling one another like seniors at their class portrait, they smile and frown across the street space. Even the old carriages and upright cars have more face than the sleek, low autos of today. Face makes the city more social, more alive. It's something very different from the graph-paper facades or hulky robotic presences of many of Boston's recent office towers (which people often call faceless).

But the new Boston has its advantages, too. In the past people surely choked on the dust and muck of these streets. Some froze in basements that flooded regularly before the great pumping stations were built. They gagged behind their gay awnings in roasting, unvacuumed summer rooms. They were driven to desperation by the unimaginable equine traffic jams. And although they enjoyed, one feels sure, lots of unintended street theater, there was little urban drama;

people were always calling Boston dowdy and dull. Now the new towers crash against the fine-grained buildings of the past. If there's a loss in continuity in the arrival of the John Hancock in Copley Square, there's a big gain in excitement.

This book is the result of a herculean labor by Peter Vanderwarker. It's an illustrated primer on cities, how to make them and how not to make them. Rightly used, along with the similar books coming out on other American cities, it will be of permanent value.

INTRODUCTION

Boston Then and Now is a book of comparative photographs which document the growth of the city from 1850 to 1980. Old and new photographs of precisely the same sites are paired to show the nature and extent of the changes that have happened in Boston.

Almost 60 old views were selected from among thousands of pictures of Boston in the collections of the Boston Public Library, the Bostonian Society and the Society for the Preservation of New England Antiquities. Views were selected which had both high photographic quality and high potential for exhibiting change.

There is a wealth of carefully executed old photographs of Boston. Two architectural photographers whose work was of particular excellence were T. E. Marr and Josiah Johnson Hawes. Marr's prints date from 1900 to 1920 and his signature can be seen in the lower right corner of the print on page 24. His work is characterized by sharp lines, clean tones and sensitive composition. Hawes (pp. 32, 84), whose images are circular, the true shape of an image emerging from the rear of a photographic lens, was an accomplished early photographer. Although he was active until 1900, his images of Boston in this book were done in the 1850s, on glass-plate negatives coated with photosensitive emulsion. He was a founder of the daguerreotype studio of Southworth and Hawes, and for many years he worked at 8 Tremont Row. His beautiful prints are like windows looking back to the Boston of 130 years ago. Great care was taken when copying the old photographs to preserve detail and to retain a sense of the tonality of the original. In some cases, the overall clarity of old images has been improved by careful copy work.

Several techniques were used to make sure that the old and new views matched exactly. The primary task was to locate the exact point from which the old view had been taken. Since the city has changed so much, many of the old vantage points no longer exist. I was often dismayed to find a beautiful old view completely obliterated by a huge new office tower. Often, getting the camera to the old vantage point required hanging out of windows or gaining access to old and sometimes precarious rooftops.

Once at the point, I selected the proper lens and the view-camera movements used to duplicate the perspective effects of the old view. To keep the views as faithful to each other as possible, care was taken not to include anything outside the frame of the old view. In the darkroom the two images were optically projected one over the other at the proper magnification—a process that allowed a close check on our efforts.

It is a shame that photography did not exist until 220 years after Boston was settled. However, much can be said about the changes shown in the photographs. Boston's topographic history is the most basic determinant of change in the city, and is the subject of an excellent book by Walter M. Whitehill. The town was originally settled on a peninsula joined to the mainland at the south by Roxbury Neck, a thin strip of land near where the views on pages 28 and 30 were taken. As the city grew, land was filled on all sides of the peninsula, forming areas now known as Back Bay, the North Station area and South Cove. The Great Fire of 1872 leveled a huge section of the downtown and waterfront, but these areas were rebuilt within a few years in much the same style.

Architectural styles change from view to view in the book. Boston is a great city architecturally: landmark buildings of many styles exist in the city from early Federal to the latest and best examples of the modern movement. The strength of both the new and the old photographs in this book lies in the dramatic juxtaposition of buildings from different ages and different styles. Few cities in the world can boast such a richness.

The shape and quality of the streets, buildings and open spaces in Boston have changed. The automobile and urban renewal have been the two strongest forces of change in the twentieth century. The old Boston was a city of narrow streets filled with people, horses and carriages, punctuated by small open spaces and surrounded by finely textured masonry buildings of eight stories or less. Today one sees wide streets filled with automobiles, punctuated by huge plazas in front of smooth, monumental, 30-to-60-story buildings.

From 1960 to 1970, the average height of buildings dominating the skyline of Boston jumped from 15 stories to 35 stories. One wonders whether all the new tall buildings built in this period will stand the test of time. Will the effort that created Government Center in the 1960s be as beneficial in time to come as the effort that had created the Back Bay 100 years earlier?

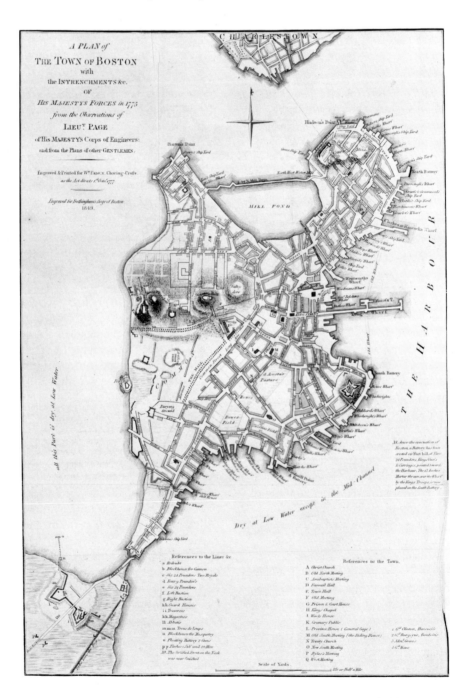

Three maps of Boston, dating from 1775 (above), 1826 (opposite, top) and 1902 (opposite, bottom), document the changes in the city's topography, the most dramatic being the landfill of Back Bay.

Aerial View of Boston, ca. 1860

The extraordinary picture of Boston in 1860, the first successful aerial view taken in the United States, was surely a technical feat for its time. Washington Street stretches diagonally across the bottom of the view, with the Old South Meetinghouse visible on the left edge. From the Meetinghouse, Milk Street can be clearly seen curving toward the water. Extending in an almost parallel arc, near the center of the picture, is Franklin Street. Ten years after this picture was taken virtually everything in the view burned to the ground. The Great Fire of 1872 stopped just short of Old South, which is still visible, but everything in the photograph to the right of Milk Street and above Washington Street burned to the ground—even the docks visible in the distance.

Aerial View of Boston, 1981

Old South can still be seen today, and the arced paths of Milk and Franklin Streets are clear. No buildings except Old South remain from the old view, grim evidence of the Great Fire. The tall building at the top center is the Shawmut Bank. Behind it to the left is One Post Office Square, and in the upper right-hand corner is the First National Bank of Boston. One small cruise boat and a small group of pleasure boats are all that are visible of the once-busy port of Boston.

Faneuil Hall from the South Market Building, 1920

Faneuil Hall, given to the town of Boston by the merchant Peter Faneuil in 1740, was designed by John Smibert, a painter, and completed in 1742. Destroyed by fire in 1761, it was rebuilt in 1762 and enlarged to its present dimensions in 1806 by Charles Bulfinch. It has continued to be a market and meeting hall since it was built, and has functioned as the town center for Boston over the years. In 1824, the hall was painted a light portland stone color to match the granite of the Quincy Market buildings adjacent to it. Behind and to the right of Faneuil Hall is the Blackstone block, which contains some of the oldest streets in the city and buildings dating from the seventeenth century. Before the Quincy Markets were built, the town dock was in this area, and ships were able to tie up within a few hundred feet of the center of Boston. This view was taken from the top floor of the South Market Building.

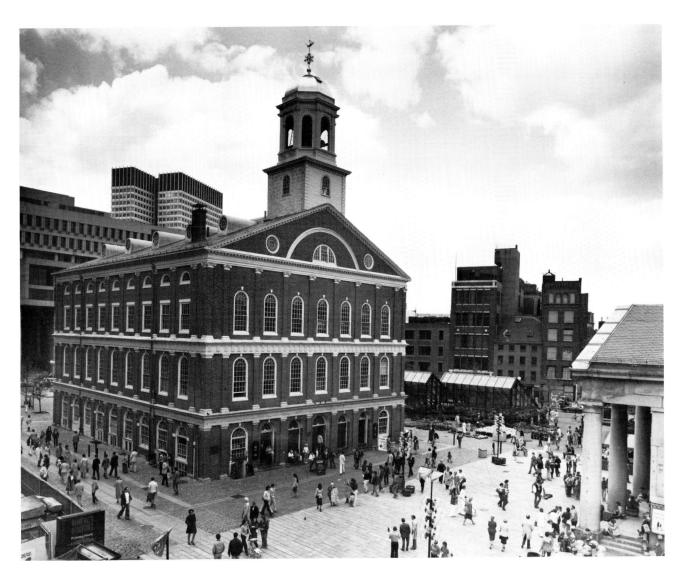

Faneuil Hall from the South Market Building, 1980

Today the restored Faneuil Hall welcomes thousands of tourists each year. Behind the hall on the left is the new City Hall, completed in 1969, and the two tall towers of the John F. Kennedy federal office building. Some of the buildings in the Blackstone block remain. Neither wagons nor automobiles make their way through the plazas surrounding Faneuil Hall today. Crowds of people, however, fill these spaces day and night, shopping in fashionable stores and eating in the dozens of restaurants which now make up the marketplace.

The Arlington Street Church, from Boylston Street, 1862

The Arlington Street Church was the first public building built in the newly filled-in Back Bay. In 1859, the Unitarian Church, which had been located on Federal Street in downtown Boston, bought the lot at the corner of Boylston and Arlington Streets and selected Arthur Gilman as its architect. The style is similar to eighteenth-century English churches, particularly St. Martin-in-the-Fields in London, designed by James Gibbs. The spire, which rises 170 feet, is supported on a base of granite. The entire building rests on 999 piles driven into the soft fill of Back Bay. The brownstone of which the church is built came from Newark, New Jersey.

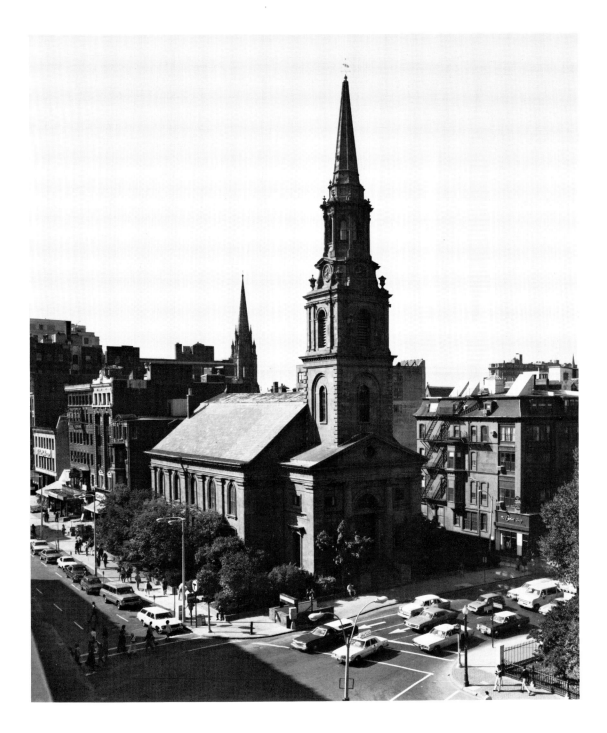

The Arlington Street Church, from Boylston Street, 1979

Today the church remains and Boylston and Arlington Streets are busy commercial districts. The spire of the Church of the Covenant (1867) is behind and to the left of the Arlington St. Church. The Ritz Carlton Hotel is just off the right edge of the picture. At the far right in the foreground is a corner of the Public Garden.

Trinity Church from Boylston Street, ca. 1903

When it was completed in 1877, Trinity Church was one of the most ambitious ecclesiastical building projects in the country. Built of Dedham granite and brownstone, it was designed by H. H. Richardson. The building is in the form of a Latin cross with a huge central tower rising 211 feet on four huge piers. The west porch and its towers were added in 1897. Like other churches in Back Bay, Trinity is supported on piles (4,500) driven into the gravel that forms the Back Bay landfill. The first major building on Copley Square, it was consecrated in 1877 and was soon joined by the Museum of Fine Arts (at the far right) and the Boston Public Library, directly opposite the church (not visible in this view). By 1895, Copley Square was surrounded by more architecturally significant buildings than any other public square in the United States.

Trinity Church from Boylston Street, 1980

Trinity Church has recently been sandblasted and much of the beauty of its contrasting stonework restored. It stands today surrounded by very different neighbors. The first John Hancock Tower, built in the late 1940s, stands behind and to the left of the church. The vertical rectangular grid of the new John Hancock Tower rises in the center of the picture and the Copley Plaza Hotel stands on the site of the old Museum of Fine Arts. The square itself was redesigned in a competition held in 1965, which was won by Sasaki, Dawson and DeMay.

Copley Square, ca. 1896

This view shows Copley Square during the height of its architectural development. The arches on the left belong to New Old South Church, Trinity Church stands in the center, and on the far right is the Museum of Fine Arts, built in 1876 by Sturgis and Brigham. The Museum was a flamboyant design, done in Gothic Revival style with pointed arches, gables, dormers and pinnacles. It was also one of the first American buildings to employ terra-cotta for exterior decoration, using panels manufactured in England.

Copley Square, 1979

Copley Square has been changed most dramatically by the addition of New England's tallest building, the 60-story John Hancock Tower, completed in 1976. In 1912, after the museum had moved to its present site in the Fenway, the Copley Plaza Hotel was built on the site. The cornice of the Boston Public Library is visible on the extreme right edge of the frame.

Copley Square, ca. 1889

In the foreground are the foundations of the Boston Public Library, designed by McKim, Mead & White, and built from 1888 to 1895. It was intended that the new library be the most architecturally significant in the country. McKim's design, based on the Renaissance palaces of Rome, was a major departure from the heavier Gothic buildings in the Square (most notably New Old South Church and the Museum of Fine Arts). The churches included in this view are (from left) New Old South Church (1875), First Baptist Church (1871) with its short, pyramidal tower, the Church of the Covenant (1867), Park Street Church (1809) farthest in the distance, Arlington Street Church (1861) and Trinity Church (1877).

Copley Square, 1979

In the foregound is the slate roof of the Boston Public Library Addition (1971), designed by Philip Johnson with the same exterior dimensions as the old Boston Public Library, the roof of which is visible directly behind. Boylston Street has been widened and serves as the main traffic artery from Back Bay to the downtown area. The new campanile of New Old South Church can be seen on the left and the John Hancock Tower is on the right. Boston's skyline is no longer punctuated by pointed spires, but by boxlike masses of downtown office buildings.

Looking Southwest at the Corner of Newbury and Dartmouth Streets, 1885

Many different building styles flourished during the period of major construction between 1860 and 1895. Most buildings were constructed in styles popular in Europe at the time. The Boston Art Club, in the center of this view, is a good example of the Queen Anne style. Designed by William Ralph Emerson in 1881, it is richly ornamented with cut brick, stone quoins, a hexagonal tower and Romanesque arched entrances. Immediately to the left is Cummings and Sears's New Old South Church, with the tall Gothic tower and contrasting stonework. The pair of buildings forms a fascinating composition of architectural massing.

*Looking Southwest at the Corner of Newbury
and Dartmouth Streets, 1980*

Both buildings still stand today, no longer isolated, but part of the overall fabric of Back Bay. The Boston Public Library can be seen in the distance on the left; the 50-story Prudential Tower rises in the distance to the right.

New Old South Church from Copley Square, ca. 1900

In 1875 the Third Congregational Church moved from Old South Meeting
House and joined other churches that had built in the Back Bay. Cummings and
Sears designed the new church in the North Italian Gothic style with character-
istic contrasting stonework and polychrome decoration.

New Old South Church from Copley Square, 1979

At first glance it appears that little has changed, but closer inspection reveals that the tower has been replaced. The original wooden pile foundation proved insufficient in the soft fill of the Back Bay, and the tower began to settle unevenly soon after completion. By 1889, it was 16¾ inches from true vertical. Work on the Boylston Street subway tunnel further aggravated the situation. By 1931, it leaned 21 inches, and the decision was made to demolish the original tower and start anew. The new steel-frame tower closely resembles the original, although it falls 15 feet short of the original 236-foot height. Today's view also shows the relation of New Old South Church to the Boston Public Library, across Boylston Street.

Boylston Street from Tremont Street Looking toward Back Bay, 1901

A circus street parade wends its way down Boylston Street. Boston Common and the Public Garden are on the right; the spires of Boston's Back Bay churches rise in the background. At the center of the picture is the Gothic clock tower of the Boston and Providence Railroad station, built by Peabody and Stearns in 1872. To the right of it one sees Trinity Church and New Old South Church (1875), both located in Copley Square. Farther to the right are the Arlington Street Church (Arthur Gilman, 1859–61), the Church of the Covenant (Richard M. Upjohn, 1865–67) and the First Baptist Church (H. H. Richardson, 1870–72). At the lower left corner is the Hotel Pelham, built in 1857. The vacant lot with the construction under way is the site of the first Boston Public Library, dedicated in 1858 and demolished in 1899. Haddon Hall is visible at the far right.

Boylston Street from Tremont Street Looking toward Back Bay, 1980

Boylston Street has grown in 80 years. Today the Colonial Building stands on the site of the Boston Public Library. Immediately above the Colonial are the old and new Hancock Towers. The light-toned building with the cupola, in the center, is the New England Life Insurance Company (1940). At the right is the Ritz-Carlton Hotel (1927) with a new addition under construction.

School Street, East from the Corner of Province Street, ca. 1865

The view shows School Street below the Parker House. In the center is the Second Universalist Church, demolished in 1872. On the right is the Boston Five Cents Savings Bank, built in 1858.

School Street, East from the Corner of Province Street, 1980

Much of the land occupied by the old Boston Five was taken when Province Street was widened in 1920. The present home of the bank now stands on the site of the Universalist Church and was designed in 1925 by the Boston firm of Parker, Thomas, and Rice. A concrete and glass addition, designed by Kallmann, McKinnell and Wood in 1972, is just visible to the left of the bank. At the end of School Street is the Old South Building and, in the distance, the tower of the Shawmut Bank.

Tremont Street from 120 Boylston Street, ca. 1901

This winter view of Tremont Street was taken looking toward the Park Street Church, visible at the left center. Boston's subway system, the first in the United States, opened in 1897, and connected Boylston Street with Park Square. The box-shaped kiosks visible in the foreground drew much criticism, and were described as being in bad taste and looking like mausoleums. The Masonic Building, far right, was dedicated on December 28, 1899. It was designed by George F. Loring and Sandford Phipps.

To the left of the Masonic Temple is the Head Building, at 181 Tremont Street, built toward the very opening of this century. Two buildings to the left is the mansard roof of the Knickerbocker Building. To its left, at the center of the photograph, is a low building with a white flagpole, the entrance to the Tremont Theatre. Designed by J. B. McElfatrick and Sons, it was completed in 1889. To the left of the theater is the Evans Building, erected in 1870.

Tremont Street from 120 Boylston Street, 1980

The Masonic Temple remains, as does the Evans Building. The Tremont Theatre, now called the Astor, was remodeled in 1949 by William Riseman and Assoc. In the distance, at the left center is the Suffolk County Court House Annex, and to its right is the 40-story tower at One Beacon Street. The spire of the Park Street Church is hidden by taller buildings erected on Tremont Street since 1920. The tall building with the balconies on two sides is Tremont-on-the-Common, built in 1965.

Boston Common and Tremont Street from Boylston Street, ca. 1915

To the left of center is the gold dome of the State House. The Park Street Church is right of center. An almost continuous row of awnings along Tremont Street protected pedestrians from sun and rain. Near the right edge of the view, with a flagpole and pennant, stands the Boston Herald Building, demolished in 1966. Midway between the Herald Building and the Park Street Church, a small cupola marks the entrance to Keith's Theatre, designed by J. B. McElfatrick, and one of the finest early American vaudeville theaters. In the foreground is Boston Common, totaling 45 acres. It was purchased by the town of Boston in 1634 from Rev. William Blackstone, making it the oldest urban park in the United States. The Common was once used to pasture cattle and to train military companies.

Boston Common and Tremont Street from Boylston Street, 1980

Large structures such as Tremont-on-the-Common now dominate Tremont Street. Below Tremont-on-the-Common, the entrance to the B. F. Keith Theatre, now named the Savoy, has been remodeled. Although the interior is preserved, the present street entrance possesses none of the former elegance. Two huge marble wings were added to the State House in 1914–17. Above the State House are a pair of State Office Buildings, the Saltonstall Building and the McCormack Building.

Tremont and School Streets, Looking South, ca. 1920

On the left is King's Chapel, the first Episcopal church in New England. A wooden church was first erected here in 1689, and the present structure was built in 1754 from plans by Peter Harrison. Across School Street is the Parker House, one of Boston's hotels. This extravagant French-château style building was built in 1884 as an addition to the original white marble structure, located down School Street (not visible). A sculpted figure of a panther can be seen springing from the high central chimney near the top of the picture. Farther down Tremont Street, with the shallow gabled roof, is the Tremont Temple, erected in 1894.

Tremont and School Streets, Looking South, 1980

King's Chapel remains the same, with the exception of a wooden balustrade added above the portico. The new 14-story Parker House, built in 1927, was designed by G. Henri Desmond. Although the interior is finished in fine hardwoods with ornate plaster decorations, the exterior retains none of the exuberance of the former building. Tremont Temple still stands, and the texture and massing of Tremont Street are much the same as 60 years ago.

South on Tremont Street from Hollis Street, 1869

The area pictured here is located near the thin neck of land that connected the original peninsula of Boston proper to the Roxbury mainland. It was not until around the time of this photo that the Back Bay began to be filled and the city began to assume its present shape. The area pictured here was settled only sparsely in the middle of the eighteenth century, with a few scattered houses and many trees. A new Congregational meetinghouse was built on Hollis Street in 1732, but the area remained largely rural in character. This rural nature is still evident in this 1869 view, which shows small wood-frame buildings at a time when Boston was growing at a rapid rate—from a population of 137,000 in 1850 to 342,000 in 1875.

South on Tremont Street from Hollis Street, 1980

Today one sees an area of Boston still in the process of change. The Massachusetts Turnpike cuts through the city in the distance, and large amounts of vacant land exist in areas near the turnpike. On the right is the Bradford Hotel; in the distance are high-rise apartment buildings built near the turnpike.

North from the Corner of Tremont and Hollis Streets, ca. 1869

This view was taken at the same time and place as the previous antique photograph, and one can see the continuation of the sign "John Street, Painter" from one view to the next. The buildings become more substantial as they progress up the street toward the Common and Boylston Street in the distance. Building materials change from wood to brick and stone. The Hotel Pelham is the structure farthest from the camera; it was moved 15 feet when the street was widened in 1869.

North from the Corner of Tremont and Hollis Streets, 1980

Tremont Street is now the main artery from downtown to the South End. The area around Hollis Street is Boston's theater district, which is being revitalized. On the left the entrance to the Shubert Theatre is getting a new coat of paint, and on the far right is the marquee of the Music Hall. Just to the left of the M in Music Hall, one can see the dome of the State House on Beacon Street. To the left of the dome the 12-story Little Building stands on the site of the Pelham Hotel.

East on Boylston Street to Tremont Street, ca. 1865

This photograph by J. J. Hawes shows the original Boston Public Library, with its tall arched windows, shortly after its completion. It served from its opening on New Year's Day, 1858, until the present library at Copley Square was completed in 1895. At the corner of Tremont Street is the Hotel Pelham, and directly across Tremont part of the John Quincy Adams house can be seen.

East on Boylston Street to Tremont Street, 1980

The old Boston Public Library has been replaced by the ten-story Colonial Building, which contains one of Boston's major theaters. Farther down the street, the Hotel Pelham has been replaced by the Little Building, one of the most prestigious office buildings erected in the early 1900s. It features a direct subway access, bay windows and an interior arcade of shops. In 1897 the John Quincy Adams house was replaced by the Hotel Touraine, which operated until the 1960s as a hotel and has now been converted to apartments. All the buildings in this view were erected around the turn of the century and have a similarity that helps to unify the block. Architectural features such as Chicago-style windows, rusticated facades and applied columns add to their richness.

Looking South at Pemberton Square, ca. 1935

Pemberton Square has seen a dramatic change in scale and style since its creation in the 1830s. This view (looking in the opposite direction to the previous two) shows the square after most of the brick townhouses had been displaced by office buildings. The street in the lower-left corner leads down the hill to Scollay Square. At the end of the square is the Houghton Dutton store, which also opened onto Tremont Street. To the left of the store is the Carney Building, followed by two low brick townhouses and the Pemberton Building, designed by Fehmer and Page, on the corner.

Looking South at Pemberton Square, 1980

Today the change in the square is dramatized further by the 40-story tower at One Beacon Street, rising in the center of the photograph. Two stories have been added to the courthouse in the form of a mansard roof. The office buildings opposite the courthouse have been replaced by the Center Plaza Office Building (1968).

Park Street Church, 1860s

Park Street Church, ca. 1890

Nine members of the Old South Church, which was the only evangelical Congregational church in Boston, split from the parent church in a revival movement and formed a new Congregational organization. They built the Park Street Church from designs by Peter Banner in 1809, at a cost of $50,000. The column capitals were carved by Solomon Willard. The church has had a colorful history: gunpowder was stored in the basement during the War of 1812 and William Lloyd Garrison spoke here against slavery before the Civil War. The elm trees in front of the church were planted in 1762 by Captain Adino Paddock, a wealthy carriage builder and leading loyalist during the Revolution. He left the city when the British evacuated in 1776. The trees were cut down in the 1880s to make room for the new street railways.

Before the subway was opened in 1897, horse-drawn and electric trolleys, seen in this view, were used to connect Scollay Square and Boylston Street. The beginning of these forms of public transportation signaled a change in the character of the streets of the city. In the distance, at the right of the picture, is the Albion Building, built in 1888 from designs by Cummings and Sears. The building was demolished in 1904.

Park Street Church, 1979

The church still stands as a graceful landmark at the center of Boston. To the rear of the church is a ministries building built in the 1960s. The 40-story tower of One Beacon Street looms behind the church. The trolleys have been replaced by buses. The Park Street station subway headhouse (built in 1897) is on the left and two new angular steel headhouses can be seen on the right; the construction for a third is under way in the right foreground.

North up Tremont Street, to Park Street, ca. 1900

A winter view shows Tremont Street, with Boston Common on the left and Park Street Church in the center. At the right is the Shreve, Crump and Low building, designed by Winslow and Wetherall and built in 1890 at the corner of Tremont and West Streets. Farther up Tremont Street a flag flies on the top of the R.H. Stearns Store. The headhouses for the Park Street subway stop are also visible.

North up Tremont Street to Park Street, 1979

The Shreve, Crump and Low building still stands, its lower two floors occupied by Papa Gino's Pizza Parlor. The subway headhouses are obscured by recent planting and tourist booths on Boston Common. Behind Park Street Church stands One Beacon Street. The McCormack State Office Building is on the left edge of the view.

North up Park Street to Beacon Street, ca. 1900

Park Street was developed soon after Charles Bulfinch's State House was dedicated in 1798. The new seat of government attracted many private houses, which were built along Park Street facing Boston Common (left). Bulfinch himself designed a row of four brick townhouses midway up Park Street. In 1809, the Park Street Church (right) was built at this lower end of Park Street, from plans by the English architect Peter Banner, on the site of a large granary. After these buildings on the east side of Park Street were completed, there had been little change when this view was taken.

North up Park Street to Beacon Street, 1980

Today one sees many of the same buildings that existed 80 years ago. The State House was enlarged in 1917. The church and houses on Park Street remain, but the Park Street Church Rectory, designed by F. A. Stahl, was built in 1968.

Province Street at Bosworth Street, ca. 1890

The steps on the left were originally part of a mansion which housed Royal Governors in the eighteenth century. Province House, as it was called, was torn down by 1825, and Bosworth Street was laid out where the gardens once were. The ornamental gate's lantern originally was lighted by oil; in this view, by gas jet. At the end of Province Street, dead center in the photo, is the Boston City Hall, built in 1865 by Gridley J. Fox Bryant and Arthur Gilman.

Province Street at Bosworth Street, 1977

Today the impact of the automobile is apparent. The street has been widened and a large parking garage added. The historic steps remain, and one can still see Old City Hall (now restored) at dead center. The tall building rising above it is the Boston Company Building, designed by Pietro Belluschi and built in 1970.

West up School Street to Tremont Street, ca. 1900

This photograph shows many of the details and textures that characterized late Victorian Boston, including ornate window pediments, mansard roofs, rusticated stonework, richly detailed cornices, gas lanterns on the street and at the entrances to major buildings, and cobblestone streets with granite cross-walks. The original Parker House of 1854 is visible, immediately above the wagon parked crosswise on School Street, as well as the ornate addition of 1888 next to it on the uphill side. In the right foreground is the plaza in front of Old City Hall, and beyond it is King's Chapel, built in 1754. Above King's Chapel and across Beacon Street is the Albion Building, built in 1888 by Cummings and Sears.

West up School Street to Tremont Street, 1980

Today much of the nineteenth-century texture and rich detail is gone. The new Parker House was built in 1927, and although the Old City Hall and King's Chapel still remain, the Albion Building has been replaced by an office tower at One Beacon Street. The Tremont Building, built in 1895, can be seen in the direct center of both views, as can 8 Beacon Street, the building seen to the left.

South at the Corner of Tremont and Winter Streets, ca. 1880

Tremont Street has been one of Boston's vital commercial streets for many years. This view shows some of the goods and services offered on the commercial streets of old Boston: hats with French styling, made-to-order shirts, textile trimmings and laundry services. Much attention is given to the display of the goods. The cast-iron railing in the foreground bears elaborate decoration.

South at the Corner of Tremont and Winter Streets, 1980

Tremont Street remains commercial in nature. Winter Street extends off to the left and leads down to Washington Street and the Downtown Crossing, which is the heart of Boston's shopping district. The building on the corner was designed by John A. Fox in 1887. Farther down Winter Street, with flagpoles, are the only two buildings surviving from the earlier photo.

South on Tremont Street toward Park Street Church, ca. 1858

Although many of the photographs printed before 1890 have faded and lost much of their original tonality, they still capture the feeling of Boston's early streets. On the left is King's Chapel. The tall building to the left of center is the original Tremont Temple, built in 1852 after designs by William Washburn, which burned in 1870. To the right is Isaiah Roger's Greek Revival Tremont House, built in 1828 and one of the most famous hotels of its day. Park Street Church is in the distance to the right of center. The street appears deserted, but was probably bustling with activity when the photograph was made. Old photographic emulsions required exposures of several minutes, and people moving on the sidewalks appear on the final print only as dark blurred shadows.

South on Tremont Street toward Park Street Church, 1980

Tremont Street was widened in 1869 and today carries three lanes of traffic from Government Center south to the Common and out through the South End. On the right is the Tremont Building, built in 1895–96 by Winslow and Wetherell. King's Chapel and the Tremont Temple are visible still, as is the Park Street Church.

*North on Washington Street from Old South Church
toward State Street, ca. 1890*

The view was taken during construction of two major buildings which still
stand along State Street. On the left is the Ames Building, designed by Shepley,
Rutan and Coolidge in 1889; on the right is the Exchange Building, 1891, by
Peabody and Stearns. At the center of the picture, directly beneath the American flag, is the cupola of the Old State House. The Boston Globe building is
immediately to the right of the State House, and to the right of the Globe can be
seen the light facade of the Boston Advertiser. Across the street, with the
pointed tower, stands the Herald Building, another member of Newspaper Row.
The Old Corner Bookstore is in the lower left corner.

North on Washington Street from Old South Church
toward State Street, 1980

Many changes have occurred along Washington Street. The Exchange Building is obscured, but the cornice of the Ames Building can be seen poking between the two tall buildings at the left of the photograph (Boston Company Building on the left, and New England Merchants National Bank, center). The third tall building (on the right) is 60 State Street (1979). In the spot formerly occupied by the Globe and the Advertiser buildings one can see a parking lot, which will be the site of Devonshire Place, designed by Steffian Bradley Associates, to be completed in 1982. In the foreground is the Old South Building (1903).

South on Washington Street from Milk Street, 1876

This photograph was taken during the centennial celebration of 1876. The entire left side of Washington Street had been destroyed in the fire of 1872; the only facade left was that of the Macullar, Williams and Parker Building, the tall structure to the left of center with the projecting cornice. The rapid rebuilding of the burned-out area accounts for the similarity of styles along the east side of the street. The newer buildings were framed in iron instead of wood and much more attention was paid to fireproof construction. The right (west) side of Washington Street, where one can see some of the older brick buildings with wooden shutters, survived the fire.

South on Washington Street from Milk Street, 1980

Washington Street has changed completely. The area declined during the 1950s and 1960s, in part because shoppers were being attracted to suburban shopping malls. F. W. Woolworth Company took a gamble in 1965 when it built the store and garage visible in the center of this picture, and Washington Street has steadily improved over the last ten years. Filene's and Jordan Marsh have stayed and built new stores, and a huge new shopping complex is planned farther down the street at Lafayette Place. The city installed the steel-and-glass canopy that protects the sidewalks on the right side of the street, and automobile traffic has been restricted so that shopping is much easier.

North from Chauncy Street toward the Post Office,
November 22, 1872

This view, taken eleven days after the Great Fire devastated Boston, shows the extent of the devastation. The burned area extended from Washington Street (left) to the water (far right) and from Summer Street almost as far as Milk Street. Some of the buildings that survived the fire are clearly visible in this view: City Hall on the far left, the spire of Old South Meeting House to its right and, to the left of center, the Post Office, its roof still under construction.

North from Chauncy Street toward the Post Office, 1980

The devastation visible in the foreground of the modern view was not caused by fire, but by the demolition of buildings to make way for Lafayette Place, a new shopping complex. Old South Meeting House is hidden, and the Post Office has been replaced by a 1933 building visible exactly in the center of the view. To the right of the Post Office is the tower of the Shawmut Bank, and just to the right of the Shawmut a steel frame rises at One Post Office Square on the site of the Old Federal Reserve Bank. The large, low brick building in the center of this view is the Jordan Marsh Department Store.

West at the Corner of Washington and Summer Streets, ca. 1910

The photograph of Boston's shopping district at the turn of the century shows three buildings on the corner, all occupied by Filene's Department Store. On the left is the Ditson Building, built in 1900 for the Ditson Music Publishing Company. Next to it on the right are two smaller commercial buildings, also taken over by Filene's. The sign over the facade of the two buildings reads "Filene's Baby to Miss Annex." Winter Street extends up to Boston Common on the right, where one can see one of the headhouses for the Tremont Street subway. Also visible are the trolley tracks and overhead wires for the Washington Street Railway, built in 1900.

West at the Corner of Washington and Summer Streets, 1980

The Ditson Building remains. The sign between the fourth and fifth floors, obscured by the Filene's sign in the old view, reads "Founded by Oliver Ditson 1840." The new 12-story building visible up Winter Street is the Provident Institution. On the right is the Gilchrists Department Store Building. Renovated after Gilchrists went out of business in 1977, it now operates as The Corner, a group of small shops around an interior mall. The intersection visible here has been renamed the Downtown Crossing by the city and most vehicular traffic has been prohibited. The Washington Street Railway is now the Orange Line, which runs underground along Washington Street.

North from Court Street toward Bowdoin Square, ca. 1865

Scollay's Building, standing on the left edge of the photograph, was not torn down until 1871 when Court Street and Tremont Row were joined together. The Sears' Block (1848), which was adjacent to Sears Crescent, is in the center, at the corner of Court and Cornhill streets. The shops in the foreground sell a variety of items ranging from ambrotypes (made by an early photographic process) to music and jewelry. The buildings in the distance mark the intersection of Court, Howard and Sudbury Streets.

North from Court Street toward Bowdoin Square, 1980

The area is now dominated by government buildings and offices, and very little remains of the lively commercial district of 120 years ago. The Sears' Block was restored in 1969 by Stull Associates. In the distance, behind the Sears' Block, is the John F. Kennedy Federal Office Building, built in 1966 as part of the renewal of Government Center. To the left is the curved facade of One, Two and Three Center Plaza. In the center is the open space of City Hall Plaza. Howard Street no longer exists. The buildings in the distance are located on New Sudbury Street.

*North at Scollay Square from the Corner of Court
and Tremont Streets, ca. 1884*

Looking toward Bowdoin Square, we see on the lower right a statue of John Winthrop by Richard Saltonstall Greenough. In the center is the Crawford House, built in 1872 at the corner of Brattle and Cornhill Streets. The horsecars are those of the Union Railway Company, formed in 1855 to operate between Cambridge and Boston. Electric trolley cars were not introduced until 1889 and the Tremont Street subway was not built until 1895–97. Notice how many of the old buildings are covered with advertisements. This trend continued into the 1900s, as Scollay Square continued to serve as a transportation center, where advertising could be seen by many people. By the 1940s the square was famous for its colorful although transient population.

North from the Corner of Court and Tremont Streets, 1980

In 1959, the city released a plan for the redevelopment of the area, and in 1960 Edward J. Logue was brought from New Haven to Boston to act as its administrator. Logue hired the architect I. M. Pei to develop a master plan that called for the removal of 22 existing streets and established guidelines for all new buildings to be built in the area. The result is a huge open plaza ringed by large formal concrete buildings, all designed and built in the 1960s. On the left is the curve of the Center Plaza Office Building, in the center is the JFK Federal Building and on the right is the corner of the new Boston City Hall.

Southeast from Bowdoin Square toward Scollay Square, ca. 1860

Bowdoin Square and the area around it was one of the earliest fashionable residential areas in Boston. There was originally a bowling green in the location that was to become the square. One early resident was Dr. Thomas Bulfinch, who built his house there in 1724. He was the father of Charles Bulfinch (1763–1844), the architect who designed many of the significant buildings in Boston (Faneuil Hall, the State House, the Harrison Gray Otis houses).

On the right is the Revere House, which was built as a hotel in 1846 by a group of members of the Massachusetts Charitable Mechanics' Association and named in honor of the Association's first president, Paul Revere. The Hotel attracted such visitors as Presidents Fillmore, Pierce, Johnson and Grant as well as Generals Sherman and Sheridan. As more Bostonians migrated in the late 1800s to the new Back Bay, the whole area around Bowdoin Square degenerated into boarding houses.

Southeast from Bowdoin Square toward Scollay Square, ca. 1925

Gradually, Bowdoin Square suffered the same decline that occurred in Scollay Square. The Revere House has here been replaced by a garage. On the left are many small hotels covered with iron fire escapes. Note how early in the century automobile traffic was already shaping this part of Boston. In the distance rises the Custom House Tower, designed by Peabody and Stearns and built in 1913–15.

Southeast from Bowdoin Square toward Scollay Square, 1934

The scale of Bowdoin Square has here changed markedly with the construction of the New England Telephone and Telegraph Building, on the left, and with a rather monumental fire station, on the right. Most of the older buildings in the distance remain from the previous view.

Southeast from Bowdoin Square, 1980

Today the changes in scale are even more striking. Additions have been made to the Telephone Building, and the JFK Federal Tower rises behind it. The new City Hall is in the center, directly beneath the Custom House tower. The two tall buildings behind City Hall are 60 State Street and the New England Merchants Bank. On the right is the nine-story end of the Center Plaza Office Building.

Northeast from Scollay Square toward
Quincy Market and the Waterfront, ca. 1920

The curved street in the foreground is Cornhill, a delightful crescent of attached buildings that was the bookselling center of the city early in the twentieth century. The tile roof of the Scollay Square subway kiosk (1898) is visible along the bottom edge. The corner building in the foreground is the Sears' Block, and behind it is the Sears Crescent, built in 1841. In the distance, directly above the Sears' Block, is Faneuil Hall, a flag flying from its cupola. The Quincy Markets are visible behind Faneuil Hall. On the far right is the 12-story Ames Building, built in 1891 by Shepley, Rutan and Coolidge.

Northeast from Scollay Square toward
Quincy Market and the Waterfront, 1980

The modern view, taken from the roof of One Center Plaza, shows the vast City Hall Plaza created during the 1960s as part of the Government Center Development. Some charming streets were lost when Scollay Square was torn down in the 1960s. Cornhill Street no longer exists, although the Sears Crescent and Sears' Block have both been restored (1969). At the bottom left is the new Government Center subway station. City Hall faces on the plaza, and behind it are Faneuil Hall and the Quincy Markets. The tall building in the center is the New England Merchants Bank (1969), and below it and to the right is the Ames Building. Immediately to the right of the Ames Building is the Old State House at the corner of Washington and State Streets.

Scollay Square from Tremont Row, ca. 1850

This photograph, taken from an attic window on Tremont Row, visible on the right, shows Scollay Square early in its colorful history. Originally a residential neighborhood, in 1838 the square was named after William Scollay, a Scottish immigrant who owned an apothecary shop. In the distance is the original gable of the central pavilion of the Sears Crescent on Cornhill Street. The building visible in the foreground of this view, Scollay's Building, was built in 1795. Other institutions located in this block next to Scollay's Building were the Boston Athenaeum (1807–1809) and the Provident Institution for Savings (1823–1833).

By the 1840s there was a variety of establishments in the square. No. 21 Tremont Row was the dancing academy of Lorenzo Papanti; next door, at No. 19, was the office of Dr. William Thomas Green Morton, a dentist who in 1846 pioneered the anaesthetic use of ether in surgery. A few years later, No. 19 was occupied by Southworth and Hawes. Scollay's Building and its neighbors were· taken down in 1870, enlarging Scollay Square into a long, thin triangle.

Scollay Square from Tremont Row, 1980

Today, Sears Crescent alone remains, its gable roof squared off in a remodeling. The old site of Scollay's Building would be at the bottom of this view, which is taken from a point 20 or 30 feet higher than the original. Cornhill Street is now City Hall Plaza. The skylights of the Government Center subway stop are visible in the lower left corner. The Ames Building (with the spiral fire escape) is to the left of center. Across Court Street is the tall, dark tower of One Boston Place (1970); behind it and to the right is the tower of the Shawmut Bank (1975).

East from Scollay Square down Court Street
toward the State House, ca. 1910

On the left is the Scollay Square Headhouse; behind it is the Sears' Block. To the right of the Sears' Block is the Shillaber Building, designed by Cummings and Sears and built in 1875–76. Above the Shillaber Building is the Ames Building. The Old State House (1712–13, alterations by Isaiah Rogers in 1830) is visible in the distance, just to the right of center, and to its right is the Sears Building. The structure with the awnings to the right of the Sears Building is Young's Hotel, built in 1845.

This image is one of the finest of the many good architectural photographs of Boston of the period. It has a striking sense of depth, drawing the viewer's eye into the space depicted and presenting the play of light on the complex textures and forms that make a city beautiful.

East down Court Street from Three Center Plaza, 1980

The view today pales by comparison. The Sears' Block has been restored, but the Shillaber Building has been replaced by the City Bank and Trust Company. The State House and the Ames Building remain. In the upper left corner is the 35-story New England Merchants Bank, and the Boston Transcript Building is visible to the right of the State House. At the far right is the Hemenway Building, designed in 1880 by N. J. Bradley. The Sears Building was demolished in 1967, when the 40-story Boston Company Building was constructed.

*North from the Corner of Commonwealth Avenue
and Berkeley Street, ca. 1910*

The architectural styles of the Back Bay were profoundly influenced by nineteenth-century French traditions, especially the Mansard roofs. The house in the center foreground was built for Charles Minot by the architectural firm of Snell and Gregerson, who followed the French styles closely. In the distance Longfellow Bridge is under construction. Note the lack of trees in the newly filled land.

*North from the Corner of Commonwealth Avenue
and Berkeley Street, 1980*

Today the Minot house has been replaced by an eight-story apartment house, designed in 1923 by Parker, Thomas and Rice. The houses built between Beacon Street and the Charles River are now occupied by Emerson College. The tall building across the river, at the left of center, is the Middlesex County Courthouse in Cambridge. The cluster of buildings on the far right in the distance is Massachusetts General Hospital.

South at the Corner of Berkeley and Marlborough Streets, ca. 1900

The First Church of Boston, designed by Ware and Van Brunt in 1868, stands on the corner. To the left is the ten-story Haddon Hall apartment house (1894), on the corner of Berkeley Street and Commonwealth Avenue. It was the only tall building in Back Bay at that time.

South at the Corner of Berkeley and Marlborough Streets, 1980

The First Church burned in 1968, and in 1972 Paul Rudolph restored its remains and designed a new chapel addition, the angular mass seen to the right of the spire. The main stained-glass windows of the old church were lost in the fire, but the wall in which it was built and some of the charred wood frames that supported the glass are carefully preserved, serving as a graphic reminder of the former structure.

*South at the Corner of Dartmouth Street
and Commonwealth Avenue, ca. 1880*

The Vendome Hotel, shown here, was built in two sections in the late nineteenth century and quickly became Boston's most fashionable residential address. The Hotel was built in two parts; the original structure is closer to the corner. Designed by William Preston in 1871, it was a symmetrical, Second Empire French design. Ten years later J. F. Ober designed a much larger eight-story addition along Commonwealth Avenue, using white Tuckahoe and Italian marble. Although it was a commercial hotel, it had many permanent residents. The hotel had a separate entrance for ladies on Dartmouth Street. At the extreme left is the campanile of New Old South Church.

*South at the Corner of Dartmouth Street
and Commonwealth Avenue, 1980*

The Vendome became less fashionable as Bostonians continued to move out toward such suburbs as Brookline in the early 1900s. In 1970, plans were made to convert the hotel to private condominiums. Construction was begun, but in 1972 a fire caused the new construction on the left side of the hotel to collapse, claiming the lives of nine Boston firemen.

East on Commonwealth Avenue from the Algonquin Club, ca. 1888

Commonwealth Avenue and the Back Bay was Boston's most ambitious and successful experiment in urban design. The entire area of Back Bay, from Roxbury to Brookline, was a foul-smelling marsh in the 1850s, when plans were begun to fill in the area and sell residential lots. Commonwealth Avenue is the central axis of the development, the plan of which is generally attributed to Arthur Gilman. Styled after a Parisian boulevard, Commonwealth Avenue was made 200 feet wide, with a park down its center. In addition, all lots were restricted so that houses must be set back 20 feet from the property line. This view, looking toward the Public Garden, shows Exeter Street in the foreground, and the Hotel Vendome in the center. The three churches visible to the left of the Vendome are the First Baptist at Clarendon Street, Central Congregational at Berkeley and Newbury Streets, and the Arlington Street Church. To the right are Trinity Church in Copley Square, and New Old South Church.

East on Commonwealth Avenue from the Algonquin Club, 1980

The Vendome remains; one can see the ghosts of the letters spelling its name on the brick party wall. All of the churches from the old view, can be seen. Directly above the Vendome is the cupola of the New England Life Insurance Company, and, to its left, in the distance, is the silvery tower of the new Federal Reserve Building, designed by Hugh Stubbins in 1975. On both sides of Trinity Church are large buildings belonging to the John Hancock Insurance Company. The older structure with the tall mast was built in the late 1940s, and the new 60-story Hancock Tower, designed by I. M. Pei, rises out of the frames on the far right. Some of the houses on Commonwealth Avenue have been replaced by apartment buildings from the 1920s.

*East on Commonwealth Avenue from
Charlesgate West, ca. 1924*

This view shows Commonwealth Avenue at Charlesgate, where the Muddy River (on the right) flows into the Charles. In the distance is the intersection at Massachusetts Avenue, where Commonwealth makes a change of direction which was planned by Frederick Law Olmsted when he designed the Back Bay Fens in 1879. Had Commonwealth Avenue continued in a straight line from Back Bay, it would have marched right into the swampy Receiving Basin, a sewer for Roxbury and Brighton. Olmsted improved the drainage of the Muddy River and converted it into an attractive park, the Back Bay Fens. Arthur Shurcliffe, the noted landscape architect of the Charles River Esplanade, designed the bridges and balustrades over the Muddy River. On the right is the Somerset Hotel, designed in 1897 by Arthur Bowditch.

East on Commonwealth Avenue from
Charlesgate West, 1980

The Muddy River is now flanked by an automobile overpass, completed in 1970, which connects Storrow Drive wirh Boylston Street and the Fenway. West of the overpass is Kenmore Square; from there on the center of the avenue is filled with trolley tracks. The Somerset still exists, though no longer as a hotel, and in the distance are the towers of downtown Boston.

North on Park Street to the State House, ca. 1880

In 1795 the Commonwealth of Massachusetts, to acquire a site for a new state house, paid the heirs of John Hancock £4,000 for the pasture on Beacon Hill above the Common. Charles Bulfinch was chosen as the architect for the new State House, the cornerstone was laid on the Fourth of July 1795, and the building occupied in January 1798. The building's facade is a graceful restatement by Bulfinch of some of the classical buildings which he had visited in London. In 1855, the original red brick was painted yellow, and the dome was covered in gold leaf in 1874.

North on Park Street to the State House, 1980

The original design of the State House is clearer today than in the earlier view. The red brick, previously painted yellow, has been sandblasted free of paint, and Bulfinch's elegant columns, balustrades and cornices have all been painted white, contrasting nicely with the brick. Two large marble wings were added to the right and left of the building.

North to 45 and 42 Beacon Street, ca. 1860

Upper Beacon Street, developed soon after the State House was built, quickly became the location of some of the most elegant houses of the Federal Period. In this view, by J. J. Hawes, the brick house with the balustrade in the distance is No. 45, the third Harrison Gray Otis House, built in 1806 by Charles Bulfinch. This was the last of three great houses which Otis built, and he lived here until his death in 1848. The granite house in the foreground is No. 42, built for David Sears by Alexander Parris in 1819. Although designed in the Greek Revival style, the house complements its Federal neighbors.

North to 45 and 42 Beacon Street, 1980

It is remarkable that the street is so unchanged today, 120 years after the J. J. Hawes view on the opposite page. Even details such as chimney pots, dormer windows, balustrades and iron railings remain the same from one view to the other. A service entrance has been built to the sidewalk in front of the Sears House, which today is owned by the Somerset Club.

East on Mount Vernon Street, 1860

In 1795, about the time the State House was being constructed, Harrison Gray Otis arranged to purchase from John Singleton Copley, the famous portrait painter, the largest tract of undeveloped land in Boston: over 18 acres, at the price of $1,000 per acre. The group of prominent lawyers which joined Otis called themselves the Mount Vernon Proprietors, and they took lots along the north side of Mount Vernon Street. In the center is No. 55, built by Jonathan Mason, a shipping merchant, in 1804. At the left, hidden behind the trees, is No. 59, designed by Edward Shaw in 1837. Up Mount Vernon Street to the right, one can see the spire of the First Baptist Church (1853) on Somerset Street.

East on Mount Vernon Street, 1980

Mount Vernon Street has changed little over the years. The Mason house, at the center, is now a museum, and No. 59 is more clearly visible, set back from the street on the left. Many other houses on Mount Vernon Street have such setbacks, which were stipulated in the deeds when the land was originally developed. The First Baptist Church is gone, and in the distance is the tower of One Beacon Street.

Southeast at the Corner of Beacon and Park Streets, ca. 1910

The house on the corner was built in 1803–04 from plans by Charles Bulfinch. Of several Bulfinch houses built along Park Street, it is the only one remaining. The house was later divided in two by George Ticknor. The next building down Beacon Street, the Claflin Building, was designed in 1884 by W. G. Preston. It housed Boston University.

Southeast at the Corner of Beacon and Park Streets, 1980

Among the alterations done to the Amory-Ticknor house are dark Queen Anne oriel windows, a porch addition and an additional story. Unfortunately, the clean lines and graceful proportions of the original Federal facade have been obscured. Past the Claflin Building is Congregational House, and at the end of Beacon Street is the tower of One Beacon Street, designed in 1972 by Skidmore, Owings, and Merrill.

South toward Tremont Street from the State House, ca. 1910

Park Street is on the left edge of the picture, and the spire of Park Street Church is just out of view to the left. In the foreground is Boston Common; Tremont Street stretches horizontally across the middle of the picture. To the left of dead center are the Greek Revival columns and pediment of St. Paul's Cathedral, designed by Alexander Parris and Solomon Willard in 1820. It is an Episcopal church and has been the Cathedral of the Diocese of Massachusetts since 1908. Three buildings to the left of the cathedral, at the corner of Winter Street, is John Fox's building of 1887. Immediately to the right of the Cathedral is the Masonic Temple, by Richard Bond, with its twin pyramidal towers.

South toward Tremont Street from the State House, 1980

The modern view shows the enormous architectural diversity of the street. The Fox Building and St. Paul's Cathedral both remain. The Masonic Temple, however, was replaced by a large department store, R. H. Stearns, which was in business until 1978. Since then, the store has been completely remodeled into housing for the elderly. The large apartment house with the balconies is Tremont-on-the-Common, built in the 1960s.

*North Side of Beacon Street between Charles and
Arlington Streets, ca. 1886*

This view of Beacon Street is a good example of how a group of buildings
constructed during a comparatively brief period can form a strong architectural
whole. All of the houses in the photograph were built between 1828 and 1860.
On the right are the earliest, six houses built in 1828 by Asher Benjamin. The
strength of this row of fine houses comes from the fascinating variations that
occur within a group of buildings consistent in size, scale and style. Similar
architectural elements, such as bay windows, dormer windows, chimney pots,
shutters and mansard roofs, are repeated on the facades at varying intervals all
the way down the street, repetitions giving the group of houses a tremendous
richness.

*North Side of Beacon Street between Charles and
Arlington Streets, 1980*

Much of the beauty of the old view of Beacon Street is missing in the modern
view. Although the Asher Benjamin houses remain, many of the other houses
have been replaced by much taller apartment houses built early in this century.
Although the street maintains the same width as before, the buildings no longer
read as a unified mass with interesting variations, but more as a collection of
completely different structures.

Northeast from the State House, ca. 1910

This view was taken not too long after the Sturgis & Brigham rear extension to the State House (visible in the lower left corner) was completed in 1895. The column at the lower left (1898) replaced an earlier monument by Charles Bulfinch, the architect of the original State House. In the distance are the North and West Ends of Boston, and at dead center, near the horizon, is the spire of Old North Church. The large building with the flag in the foreground is the Ford Memorial Building, constructed in 1904. The rear of the Church of the New Jerusalem (1845–1964) is visible at the far right.

Northeast from the State House, 1980

Two large granite wings were added to the State House in 1914–17 by William Chapman, R. Chipston Sturgis and Robert D. Andrews; one wing can be seen at the lower right. The column remains, but the pleasant park is now a parking lot. In the center, three more government buildings have been built: the Saltonstall Building (left, 1965), the McCormick Building (center, 1975) and the Suffolk County Court House Addition (1940).

West to Back Bay, 1858 (Opposite, Top)

This view was taken from the State House, just before the ambitious plan to fill in the Back Bay was begun. The Mill Dam (which is now Beacon Street) is in the center, separating the Back Bay on the left from the Charles River on the right. The Public Garden has already been constructed, and the waterline is at Arlington Street, the first of the cross streets of Back Bay. Railway lines that crossed the Back Bay were used to carry gravel fill from Needham and Quincy. A crew of 80 men, using a steam shovel, were able to move 2,500 cubic yards of fill per day, enough to fill the area of two house lots. The newly created land was owned by the Commonwealth, which sold the lots to private owners.

West to Back Bay, 1869 (Opposite, Bottom)

By 1861, the Bay was filled to Clarendon Street, by 1871 past Exeter Street. This view shows the Arlington Street Church and the Central Congregational Church. Behind the Arlington Street Church is seen the Peace Jubilee Coliseum, built to house a musical extravaganza in 1869. The site became Copley Square ten years later. Between the two churches are the Museum of Natural History and the Rogers Building, part of MIT, on Boylston Street between Berkeley and Clarendon Streets.

West to Back Bay, 1980 (Above)

Today the development of Back Bay is complete and a cluster of tall buildings can be seen along Boylston Street. The old and new John Hancock Towers stand next to each other on the left, and immediately to the right of the new Hancock is the Christian Science Church Tower (in the distance) designed by I. M. Pei. The tall building visible directly above the Arlington Street Church is the Prudential Insurance Company Building (1965).

East from the State House, ca. 1876

This view looks from Beacon Hill across downtown Boston to the waterfront, the harbor and East Boston beyond. The First Baptist Church is at the left; just to its right is the dome of the Quincy Markets. The largest waterfront building, visible a little to the left of center, is the State Street Block, by Gridley J. Fox Bryant. A little to the right of center, with its rounded French roof, is Old City Hall, by Gridley J. Fox Bryant and Arthur Gilman. Moving to the right of City Hall, one can see two more large buildings with characteristic French mansard roofs and dormer windows: the Post Office (A. B. Mullett, 1869) and, on the far right, the Equitable Building (Arthur Gilman, 1874). The Boston Athenaeum is the large building with three skylights in the lower-right foreground.

East from the State House, 1980

Very few of the buildings in the 1876 photograph can be seen today, and the waterfront is almost entirely obscured. The tower of One Beacon Street looms largest in the center, and the twin Harbor Towers can be seen immediately to the right (I. M. Pei, 1972). To the right of Harbor Towers, Mullett's Post Office has been replaced by the Post Office and Federal Building by Ralph Adams Cram (1933). The Boston Athenaeum is almost completely obscured at the lower right.

South from the State House, 1858

This photograph continues the panorama begun in the previous photograph of 1876. Old South Meeting House on Washington Street is on the left edge, the Federal Street Church is to the left of center, and the Park Street Church spire is on the right edge. Just to the left of the Park Street Church the New York Central railroad viaduct leads from the wharf at the foot of Summer Street, curves into the harbor, and heads toward South Boston. Below the viaduct is the hipped roof of the Music Hall, built in 1852 by George Snell. The trees in the foreground mark the Old Granary Burial Ground. Almost everything in this view from the waterfront up to Washington Street burned in the Great Fire of 1872.

South from the State House, 1980

The mosaic of structures is here comprised entirely of office buildings. The oldest ones are at the bottom of the picture and date from before 1900. In the middle are many of the eight- to 15-story office structures built early in this century, such as the Paddock Building on Tremont Street, to the left of center with the white cornice. Farther away, at the top center of the view, with their characteristic trapezoidal tops, are a pair of 25-story Art Deco office buildings dating from the 1920s. Finally, stretching across the top of the picture are the tall office towers that have all been built since 1964. Although it is obscured by other buildings, the Music Hall exists today as the Orpheum, and is the oldest existing music hall in Boston.

West up Milk Street to Washington Street, 1876

The buildings on the left in the picture were brand-new at the time—the entire block having burned in the Great Fire of 1872. After the fire, many of the buildings were rebuilt in time for the Centennial celebration of 1876 (notice the Centennial Lunch Room, far left). The building with the flagpole is the Goddard Building (1873–74), by N. J. Bradlee and W. T. Winslow. The building in the center, most heavily draped with bunting, is the Boston Post Building, by Peabody and Stearns, built on the location of the birthplace of Benjamin Franklin. Next door, at the corner of Washington Street, is the Transcript Building by Gridley J. Fox Bryant and Louis Rogers (1873).

West up Milk Street to Washington Street, 1980

Today the Transcript Building and cast-iron Boston Post Building remain, although the upper floors of the Transcript Building are in disrepair. A bust of Benjamin Franklin is located under a small arch between the second and third floors of the Post Building. The Goddard Building was altered and two floors were added around 1930. On the right is the Old South Building (1903).

Corner of Milk and Devonshire Streets, ca. 1890

This view of 1890 was taken one block farther west on Milk Street. In the center is the International Trust Building, designed by William Gibbons Preston in 1892. Its well-proportioned facade is similar to some of the early tall buildings done in Chicago. On the left is the corner of the Equitable Building.

Corner of Milk and Devonshire Streets, 1980

The International Trust Building was enlarged in 1906, more than doubling its size. The building fell into disrepair in the 1960s, and was only recently designated a City Landmark. The building is currently being restored, but unfortunately has lost its cornice. On the left, on the site of the former Equitable Building, stands the Shawmut Bank. The next building up Milk Street is the Beacon Trust Building (1921), by A. H. Bowditch.

West from Custom House Tower, ca. 1920

This view looks west from the waterfront across the downtown area, Beacon Hill and, in the distance, Back Bay and the Charles River Basin. The large building in the center foreground of the 1920 photograph is the Exchange Building. State Street is below it to the right, ending toward the center of the picture at the Old State House (the cupola is barely visible, most of it hidden by the corner of the Exchange Building). On the far right, one can see the curved forms of Cornhill and Brattle Streets. Directly above the Old State House is the dome of Bulfinch's State House. To its left is the Park Street Church, its spire clear against the trees of the Common. To the left of the Park Street Church, in the far distance, are the spires of the churches around Copley Square. On the left edge is the mansard roof of A. B. Mullett's Post Office of 1869.

West from Custom House Tower, 1980

Today the white spire of the Park Street Church stands out clearly in the center, as does the cupola of the Old State House. To the right of it are the Romanesque arches of the Ames Building, its facade recently cleaned of years of accumulated soot. Next to the Ames Building is the 40-story tower of 60 State Street. Cornhill and Brattle Streets are replaced by Boston City Hall on the far right, and above City Hall is the curved front of One Center Plaza. Looking at Back Bay, Trinity Church can be seen dwarfed by the Hancock and Prudential Towers. On the left, the Old Post Office has been replaced by the huge granite Post Office of 1933. At dead center, one can still see the French-style roof of Old Boston City Hall.

West on Water Street toward Washington Street, ca. 1865

This photograph was taken when the area was the heart of Boston's commercial district. The buildings on the left were demolished in 1869 when Mullett's Post Office was built. Note the gas lantern, cobblestoned streets and solid granite sidewalks. On the right is the Simmons Block, built by Carl Fehmer.

West on Water Street toward Washington Street, 1980

Today Cram and Ferguson's Post Office rises on the left. In the center is the Winthrop Building, designed by Clarence Black (1893–94), Boston's first building to be framed in steel entirely. This handsome structure of warm buff brick, curved to fit its site, is a good example of the new breed of buildings that were built in the city after 1890. The Minot Building (Parker, Thomas, and Rice, 1911) is just to the right of the Winthrop Building, and on the far right is the Fidelity Building, built in Neoclassical style in 1906 by Winslow and Wetherell.

North on Devonshire Street at the Corner of Water Street, ca. 1915

Devonshire Street runs parallel to Washington Street. This view looks toward the Old State House, the end of which is visible in the distance. The buildings behind the streetlamp in the 1915 photograph are the Boston Advertiser and Boston Globe Buildings, which also front on Washington Street. On the corner is the Minot Building. Immediately left, the Winthrop Building is marked by a "To Let" sign in the window. At the far left is the Lawrence Building, also by Parker, Thomas, and Rice (1908). On the right are the columns of Mullett's Post Office.

North on Devonshire Street at the Corner of Water Street, 1980

The newspaper buildings are now gone, and in their place will rise a 37-story tower by Steffian Bradley Associates called Devonshire Place. The State House is still visible, and the tall building rising behind it is the New England Merchants National Bank (Edward Larabee Barnes, 1969). High above the Minot Building is the top of the Boston Company Building. Next to the subway station is Spring Lane, which is the location of the freshwater spring used by the first settlers of Boston.

North at Post Office Square, ca. 1910

On the left is A. B. Mullett's Post Office and Sub-Treasury, begun in 1869. The building shows the French influence typical at this time: it is heavily columned, with many arched and pedimented openings and very strong mansard roofs. The monumental sculptural groups at the top of the central pavilion were done by Daniel Chester French. In the middle of the photo is the National Shawmut Bank, built in 1906, and on the right is the Delta Building, erected on a thin triangular site.

North at Post Office Square, 1980

In 1933 Cram and Ferguson designed a new Post Office, which now occupies the site of the old one. No less monumental a building, its form was influenced by the Art Deco style of the 1920s and 1930s. The National Shawmut Building is now the home of Brown Brothers Harriman Company. In the distance are the towers of the New England Merchants Bank and 60 State Street. The large building on the right is Ten Post Office Square, built in 1929.

Up State Street from Merchant's Row, ca. 1900

In the center of the old view is the Exchange Building, built in 1891 by Peabody and Stearns and probably the largest office building of its time. State Street is visible in the foreground, running up to the Old State House, which is just out of view on the right. On the far left is the Fiske Building, erected in 1888 by Peabody and Stearns.

Up State Street from Merchant's Row, 1980

The Exchange Building is being remodeled to allow the original stone facade to remain, and a new office tower to rise behind it. One can see farther up State Street in this view, and the Boston Company Building is visible. On the far right is the corner of the India Building, built in 1902 by Peabody and Stearns.

East at the Old State House, ca. 1900

This view looks over the Old State House and up Court Street toward Pemberton Hill. In this photograph of 1900, the Old State House cupola and trim are painted in a dark shade. Behind the cupola is the light stone facade of the Sears Building, by Cummings and Sears. To the left is the Rogers Building, 1868. Both structures stand on Washington Street. At the right is the 14-story Ames Building, by Shepley, Rutan and Coolidge (1891), which dominated the Boston skyline until the Custom House tower was built in 1914.

East at the Old State House, 1980

Today, although there are much taller buildings surrounding the Old State House, there is more space immediately around this eighteenth-century landmark. The "Georgian Jewel" dates from 1712–13, but the architect is unknown. The government of the Commonwealth of Massachusetts met here until Bulfinch's State House was built in 1795. The Old State House was restored in 1881 by George A. Clough and designated a landmark by the city. The buildings in the distance, immediately to the right of the cupola, are Ashburton Place (far distance) and Center Plaza, which occupies the former site of Scollay Square. The Ames Building remains today as one of the earliest and still one of the most elegant tall buildings in Boston. The Boston Company Building (1970) now occupies the site of the Rogers Building and the Sears Building.

West up State Street to the State House, ca. '1876

This photograph was probably taken during the Centennial celebration, when the city was decorated with many flags. The State House and the Sears Building are visible at the end of State Street, which has connected the State House with the water since the earliest days of Boston, originally extending well out into the harbor along Long Wharf, built in 1710. Continuous rows of shops and warehouses lined Long Wharf, and State Street was Boston's link to the harbor and the oceans that brought the city its goods. On the right is the Richards Building (ca. 1859), an early cast-iron commercial structure.

West up State Street to the State House, 1980

The Old State House now seems like a tiny beacon when compared to the tall office towers surrounding it today. Behind it is the Boston Company Building; to the right is 60 State Street. Two stories with oriel windows have been added to the Richards Building. Most of the buildings along State Street today are in the eight- to 15-story range, compared to the four to six stories of a hundred years ago. State Street still leads to the sea, although its path is crossed by the Central Artery. At its former terminus on Long Wharf, the New England Aquarium now stands.

*The Proctor Building, Corner of Kingston and Bedford Streets,
July 28, 1903*

The building at 100 Bedford Street was designed in 1897–98 by the firm of
Winslow, Wetherall and Bigelow for the estate of Thomas E. Proctor, a promi-
nent lawyer. This commercial building is ornately decorated with a variety of
architectural motifs, and is a striking display of the nineteenth-century use of
terra-cotta. Sculptured terra-cotta facilitated the use of a wealth of architectural
motifs, such as the floral frieze and cartouches above the third floor, and allowed
windows to be constructed that would have been impossible with stone. The
ornament follows the style of the Spanish Renaissance and the building is capped
with an elaborate high copper cresting decorated with torches.

The Proctor Building, Corner of Kingston and Bedford Streets, 1980

The Proctor Building is in good condition today, although the original storefronts on the ground level have been changed. Unfortunately, at the time this photograph was taken the building was for sale and its future uncertain. Behind the Proctor Building rises 100 Summer Street and the left is the tower of the First National Bank of Boston. To the right, in the distance, is the tower of the Federal Reserve Bank.